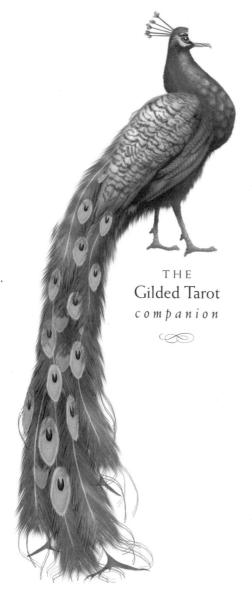

THE
Gilded Tarot
companion

About the Author

The tarot first enchanted Barbara Moore about a dozen years ago. Since then she has enjoyed studying, teaching classes, and speaking at tarot conferences around the United States. Her articles have appeared in several tarot publications, including Llewellyn's *New Worlds of Mind and Spirit* and Llewellyn's *Tarot Update*. She has sat on the *Tarot Journal* editorial board and has studied with renowned tarot scholars Mary K. Greer and Rachel Pollack. Through her position as the Tarot Specialist for Llewellyn, it has been Barbara's honor to work with the most creative authors and artists in the tarot community and vibrant tarot organizations. Sharing her love of tarot has been one of the most satisfying endeavors of her career.

About the Artist

Ciro Marchetti's professional career has included working in England, where he graduated from Croydon College of Art and Design in London. In South America, he cofounded a design studio and for several years was a parttime instructor at the Instituto Nacional de Diseño in Caracas, Venezuela. Since 1992 he has been based in Miami, Florida, where he opened the U.S. subsidiary of his design studio, Graform International, which provides a wide range of design- and marketing-related services to domestic and multinational corporations. He gives lectures in digital imagery and illustration at the Fort Lauderdale Art Institute. Visit his website at www.ciromarchetti.com.

THE

GILDED TAROT

companion

Barbara Moore

Art by Ciro Marchetti

Llewellyn Publications
Woodbury, Minnesota

FIRST EDITION
Seventh Printing, 2007

Book design and editing by Rebecca Zins
Cover and interior art © 2004 by Ciro Marchetti
Cover design by Ellen Dahl

Library of Congress Cataloging-in-Publication Data
Moore, Barbara, 1963-
    The gilded tarot companion / Barbara Moore;
art by Ciro Marchetti.—1st ed.
      p. cm.
    ISBN 13: 978-0-7387-0520-0
    ISBN 10: 0-7387-0520-9
    1. Tarot. I. Title.

BF1879.T2M652 2004
133.3'2424—dc22

                2004048338

Llewellyn Worldwide does not participate in, endorse, or have any authority or responsibility concerning private business transactions between our authors and the public.

    All mail addressed to the author is forwarded but the publisher cannot, unless specifically instructed by the author, give out an address or phone number.

    Any Internet references contained in this work are current at publication time, but the publisher cannot guarantee that a specific location will continue to be maintained. Please refer to the publisher's website for links to authors' websites and other sources.

Llewellyn Publications
A Division of Llewellyn Worldwide, Ltd.
2143 Wooddale Drive, Dept. 978-0-7387-0520-0
Woodbury, MN 55125-2989, U.S.A.
www.llewellyn.com
Llewellyn is a registered trademark of Llewellyn Worldwide, Ltd.

PRINTED IN THE UNITED STATES OF AMERICA
ON RECYCLED PAPER

Contents

Introduction

*Y*ou are about to embark on a journey. With this book and Ciro Marchetti's beautiful images as guides, you'll discover the amazing world of tarot as well as learn about yourself, your life, and your choices.

The artwork of the *Gilded Tarot* will draw you in and invite you to explore the messages hidden there. It's easy to get lost in such marvelous detail, such enchanting vignettes. This book, although lacking in the poetry of the art, may prove a useful companion, presenting practical and clear information and instructions to help you get the most out of your tarot experience.

First, you'll read about the tarot deck itself: its structure and basic meanings. Instructions for divination start from the beginning: how to ask a good question. You'll also learn about picking a significator and interpreting reversed cards. Finally, you'll see how to interpret a spread and add your own special ritual touches, if you want.

To help you develop a personal relationship with the cards and add your own layers of meaning to the standard interpretations, exercises are provided throughout the book. This is an option if you want to expand your tarot studies. If you want, though, you can read the cards using the interpretations provided.

After an overview of tarot basics, you'll learn meanings for all the cards, starting with the Major Arcana, followed by the Minor Arcana and, lastly, the court cards. The last chapter will give you a few spreads to try for yourself.

Artist's Notes

I've always been intrigued by the visual symbolism of astrology and tarot, and the theme has often appeared in my previous works. So when I received an enquiry from Llewellyn proposing the idea of creating my own tarot deck, it seemed such an appropriate project and was one in which I was immediately interested.

However, after the initial enthusiasm, it soon became apparent just how much work this would represent—not only in the sheer volume of creating seventy-eight illustrations, but in attempting to make those illustrations acceptable to the majority of the tarot community. The merit of any creative endeavor is subjective in the eye of the beholder, but—in this case—added to the mix is the extremely personal relationship between the cards and their readers.

While I owned a few decks, which I'd collected for their artistic merit years earlier, my knowledge of the subject was limited and I would obviously have to address that, but I also decided to take advantage of my lack of familiarity. As I started to read more on the subject and review numerous decks to assess their various illustrative styles, I deliberately avoided viewing more than a few cards of each deck. I wanted to be free to visualize my own personal interpretation of the message behind each card unbiased, with a minimum of preconceptions and influence from seeing the work of others.

Another early decision was to keep the approach reasonably traditional; I was amazed at the number of novelty decks available, and was quite sure I didn't want to add to them. I joined various forums and passively eavesdropped numerous topics, gradually getting a better feel for the tarot community, and came to the conclusion that there were two principal driving forces. The first was the obvious one of the deck as an instrument for reading. Did it speak to its owner? The second was the common and popular acquiring of decks as collections. In response to both, I set myself the following goals: the deck would be based on and pay homage to the Rider-Waite. Most users would therefore be immediately familiar and comfortable with it. I would make it visually attractive, both to enrich the actual reading experience and also appeal to collectors. I would incorporate a number of personal touches to ensure the deck's character was unique and not merely another Rider-Waite clone.

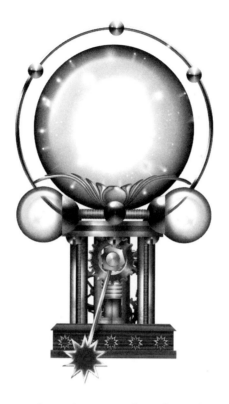

A common theme in my work is the inclusion of me-
chanical devices, and this is continued on various cards in
the Major Arcana of the *Gilded Tarot*. These machines,
which straddle the opposing worlds of science and magic,
somewhat basic in their construction and clockwork move-
ments of gears and cogs, are of an earlier time . . . while not
of the world of microprocessors and chips, they are never-
theless capable of wonders beyond today's technology.

While the tarot reveals the querent's journey, I bring attention to the stage of Mother Earth on which this story is being told. Detailed visual emphasis from trees, blades of grass, and stones, to the inclusion of a number of animals, birds, and other living creatures, reconfirm this sharing of the Earth.

In some cards their inclusion adds to the story, but in which way is up to the reader. In the Ten of Swords, the poignancy of the scene is enhanced by the approaching deer; is it conscious of what it's witnessing, and is it simple animal curiosity or a reverential acknowledgment?

The owl in the Nine of Swords not only reinforces that the scene is at night, but its forward-staring glare—which of all birds, only the owl is capable of—is slightly disturbing. What is it doing there, how long has it been there, did its arrival awaken the girl, or was it part of her dream that awoke her?

Artist's Notes
◆

The deer in the Two of Wands are not just present and aware of the man's approach, but it seems they are attentive and curiously waiting on the decision that is to be made, both by the man in the card . . . and, perhaps, by us as readers.

In the Six of Swords, the woman proceeds along her silent (secret?) journey; she looks forward with intent and purpose. Is she simply traveling to or escaping from something? Is she even aware of the toad? It most assuredly is aware of her.

In the Nine of Cups, we are greeted by the epitome of the jovial, welcoming innkeeper. Here there are good spirits in more ways than one. The barrels reconfirm abundance; even the mice playfully peering to see the cups' contents seem to reinforce the card's message of warmth and contentment.

In the Ten of Cups, we (or in this case me, the absent male figure) return home from our journey or day's work. An ideal home and family scene awaits us: mother, daughter, and a playful cat sharing a leisurely pastime. This is a scene of harmony and well-being free of conflict or strife.

The Eight of Pentacles shows the lonely apprentice at his duties, which again have extended into the night. But at least he shares the company of an unlikely friend.

Just as the silent, sometimes unnoticed animals bring an additional layer of meaning to these images, so will you, the reader, add perspectives and insights. Enjoy the journey as much as I have enjoyed creating the *Gilded Tarot*.

Artist's Notes
♦

THE
Basics

*Y*ou're probably anxious to get to know your new deck. In this section you'll find a brief introduction to the structure of the deck. This will help you understand the meanings of the cards in general terms. The later sections will help you provide more in-depth interpretation. Think of this as the outline for the card meanings. The details and nuances will come in time.

The Cards

Remember that the tarot is very personal and that the cards are packed with many meanings. Use this text as a guidebook, but let your own intuition be the final word. If something here does not make sense, discard it. Divination is not a hard science. Use the exercises provided to help flesh out the meanings that you'll use for your own readings. A journal or notebook will be especially handy in keeping all your notes and observations in order. Throughout this book, there will be exercises to help you solidify your understanding of the cards.

Seventy-eight cards may seem like a lot to learn. Dividing the deck into sections makes it easier. The first main division is in two parts: the Major Arcana (twenty-two cards) and the Minor Arcana (fifty-six cards). *Arcana* means "secrets"—so the Major Arcana are the "big secrets." In practical terms, these are the cards that represent important milestones, major changes, events beyond our control, and spiritual growth. The Minor Arcana, "lesser secrets," generally depict events, situations, or people related to everyday life. An important characteristic of the Minor Arcana is personal control—that is, they represent aspects of your life over which you have the control.

The Minor Arcana

The Minor Arcana are usually very simple to understand because most people are familiar with the structure already. Think of a pack of playing cards: four suits (clubs, hearts, spades, and diamonds), with each suit having ten pip cards numbered ace through ten and three court cards (King, Queen, Jack). The Minor Arcana is just like that, with the addition of one court card for each suit. The court cards of the tarot reflect their medieval roots: King, Queen, Knight, and Page. The suits have different names and symbols but still relate directly to the suits of playing cards [alternative names are in brackets]:

WANDS [Rods, Batons, or Staves] = Clubs

CUPS [Chalices] = Hearts

SWORDS = Spades

PENTACLES [Coins, Disks, or Stones] = Diamonds

In addition to relating to playing-card deck suits, the tarot suits are associated with the four elements. This helps define the suit's relation to our daily lives. The illustration below shows the four suits, and the list below it reveals each suit's elemental association and the aspects of life it represents.

WANDS (left). Fire or Air. Career, projects, inspiration.

CUPS (top). Water. Emotions, relationships, creativity.

SWORDS (right). Air or Fire. Challenges, intellect, ways of thinking.

PENTACLES (bottom). Earth. Physical world, money, resources.

SEVEN OF PENTACLES

THREE OF CUPS

SEVEN OF PENTACLES, TOP, AND THREE OF CUPS

The Basics

◆

4

Each Minor Arcana suit is associated with an area of life. All the cards are numbered as well; each of these numbers has meanings.

ACES: New beginnings, opportunity.

TWOS: Balance, duality, a crossroads or choice.

THREES: The full expression of the suit, achievement.

FOURS: Structure, stability, stagnation.

FIVES: Instability, conflict, loss, opportunity for change.

SIXES: Communication, problem-solving, cooperation.

SEVENS: Reflection, assessment, motives.

EIGHTS: Movement, action, change, power.

NINES: Fruition, attainment.

TENS: Completion, end of a cycle.

Using this information, you can already get a sense for a card's meaning. For example, the Seven of Pentacles could represent an assessment of resources or property. This card shows a woman looking at the fruit on a tree. She might be contemplating the work invested and comparing it to the harvest gained by that investment. The Three of Cups could indicate the achievement of relationships. This image shows three woman celebrating the joy of their friendship.

While the numbered cards show different situations of everyday life, the court cards bring personality to these situations. They can represent other people or the querent (the person asking the question). Because real people are complex, the court cards usually represent just a facet of a person—the part of the person engaged in the particular situation being inquired about.

PAGES: Novices, eager and enthusiastic but sometimes shallow; can indicate a message that the querent will receive.

KNIGHTS: Extremists, very focused (like a knight on a quest); can be unbalanced or fanatical; may represent a fast-moving situation.

QUEENS: Mature and reflective; one who nurtures others; can be prone to obsession.

KINGS: Mature and expressive; one who organizes and controls external matters, sometimes at the expense of internal or personal matters.

Exercise 1

𝒫ut your Minor Arcana cards in numerical order. Look at each one and connect the image on the card to the associations of the suit and the number as described above. Write your observations in a notebook. Note whether the connections were obvious or subtle. Also note whatever details grab your attention. Write down why a particular image intrigued you and how it affects the meaning of the card for you.

Exercise 2

𝓛ay out your court cards. Think about the personality represented on each card. Match that card with someone in your life, noting the particular behaviors, characteristics, or habits that caused the connection in your mind.

The Major Arcana

The Major Arcana are made up of twenty-two cards, numbered zero through twenty-one. Just as the minor suits have an elemental association, so does the Major Arcana; it is connected with the element of Spirit. In addition to being numbered, the Majors are also named as follows:

0 The Fool

I The Magician

II The High Priestess

III The Empress

IV The Emperor

V The Hierophant

VI The Lovers

VII The Chariot

VIII Strength

IX The Hermit

X Wheel of Fortune

XI Justice

XII The Hanging Man

XIII Death

XIV Temperance

XV The Devil

XVI The Tower

XVII The Star

XVIII The Moon

XIX The Sun

XX Judgement

XXI The World

The names give some indication of the meaning. For example, the Hermit means taking time to retreat from the world and look inward. The Star brings hope and guidance, a light to follow through otherwise dark times.

Exercise 3

*L*ist the meanings or associations that come to mind simply based on the name of each Major Arcana card.

The Fool's Journey

Just as dividing the Minor Arcana into suits and learning about the suit and numerological associations provide a brief overview and introduction to these cards' meanings, learning the Fool's journey helps introduce us to the Major Arcana. The twenty-two Major Arcana cards depict a journey through life, a journey of self-development and spiritual growth. We all start as the Fool, the first card of the Major Arcana, though all our journeys are different.

To visualize the Fool's journey, lay out the cards, placing the Fool alone at the top. Then lay out the rest of the cards, in numerical order, underneath the Fool in three rows of seven (1–7, 8–14, and 15–21).

1. The first row shows the steps we go through in our basic development from birth to young adult and in learning how to live in society.

2. The second row illustrates the universal laws or rules of society that we must confront, question, and come to terms with; it also is about discovering who we are.

3. The final row is our spiritual development.

THE FOOL: The Fool marks the beginning of the journey as an archetypal child, unformed and unlearned, innocent and eager.

THE MAGICIAN: The Magician represents the male principal or *animus*. This is our active or outgoing energy, our skills and abilities in terms of the outer world. In basic terms, it is how we do things and how we learn.

THE HIGH PRIESTESS: The High Priestess embodies the female principal or *anima*. This is our passive or introspective energy, our skills as they relate to our inner world and self-reflection. In short, this is how we think or feel about things and what we know intuitively.

THE EMPRESS: The Empress represents the Mother archetype and our experience with mothering, nurturing, emotions, and our creative impulse.

THE EMPEROR: The Emperor represents the Father archetype and our experience with authority, reason, and logic.

THE HIEROPHANT: The Hierophant is our formal education within our society, including school, religious training, and cultural traditions.

THE LOVERS: In a word, adolescence—our experience of hormones, sex, and our sense of self.

THE CHARIOT: The Chariot illustrates the ability to see both sides of an issue; it marks the ending of the "but that's not fair!" stage.

Once we have synthesized these archetypes into our sense of self, we are usually pretty well prepared to participate in society. Sometimes we incorporate some of these elements better than others. For example, if someone "has issues with her mother," she may not have dealt very effectively with the Empress.

STRENGTH: Strength is where we learn to control our instincts and impulses, where we master ourselves and develop self-control. We may want to party all night, eat the entire buffet, or shop until our credit card reaches its limit, but we realize that it is probably best if we do not indulge all these desires.

THE HERMIT: This is us feeling the need to "find ourselves." We turn inward, questioning all we've learned, and try to find a sense of inner peace.

WHEEL OF FORTUNE: Just when we feel centered and balanced, our resolve is tested by a spin of fate. Something happens beyond our control or our ability to foresee.

JUSTICE: In the aftermath of the spin of fate, we find out how we fared, and realize that we reap what we sow. If we were well prepared, we come out perhaps shaken but okay. If not, we may need to revisit the Hermit phase of the journey—or move on to . . .

THE HANGING MAN: The Hanging Man shows us the strength and power of letting go and enjoying the view from a different perspective. This card also shows us the importance of sacrifice. Some things are worth sacrificing for and maybe we really can't have it all—at least not the way we planned.

DEATH: Just when we get comfortable hanging on by a thread, we are faced with a major change in our lives. This can be any major change, positive or negative: an unexpected promotion, the ending of a relationship, moving to a new place.

TEMPERANCE: After coming through a transformational experience, we learn graceful balance and tolerance. We learn to adapt to changes in circumstance while maintaining our center, our sense of self.

We have come through a very difficult phase of our development. We have faced Death in some guise. We've learned to maintain ourselves, to adapt to circumstances, to not rail against the seeming unfairness of the universe. What more could we possibly have to do?

THE DEVIL: Balanced, strong, and confident, now we are asked to confront our shadow selves, the dark aspects of ourselves that we fear and that may control us in subtle ways. These may be aspects that we learned to control or repress in the Strength card. This worked well for a while, before we had the knowledge and experience not just to ignore and repress these aspects. Now we need to revisit them, learn to appreciate the positive qualities they can bring to our lives, and synthesize them appropriately.

THE TOWER: Although we feel we've got ourselves under reasonable control by now, the universe reminds us that we are not in control of everything. The Tower gives us a bolt from the blue that shakes our very foundation. This may differ from the Wheel or Death in that rather than disrupting the external circumstances of our lives, the Tower shakes the foundations of our belief systems.

THE STAR: The Star provides us guidance, hope, and optimism after cataclysmic events, giving us the strength we need to rebuild our crumbled foundations.

THE MOON: While the Star guides us on our way, the Moon teaches us to question everything and to realize that things are not always what they seem. By the light of the Moon, we can lose our way or be distracted by enticing shadows. We can also have inspiring dreams. We must learn to tell the difference.

THE SUN: After wandering in the Moon, we emerge into the Sun with increased strength and self-awareness, with the certainty that we know ourselves, what we believe in, and what is real.

JUDGEMENT: The Judgement card calls us to a deeper spiritual realization. Often it is a call to action, to share your knowledge or experience with others.

THE WORLD: This is the end of the cycle; we have learned all of our lessons and have achieved integration, balance, and spiritual awareness.

Exercise 4

*L*ook at each Major Arcana card. Write down a situation or experience from your own life that reminds you of each step of the Fool's journey.

Care and Storage

There are many myths and old wives' tales about tarot cards. You may have heard some of them: you cannot buy your own cards, they must be given to you; you must wrap them in silk and keep them in an oak box; you must not let anyone else touch your cards. Most people don't put much stock in these dictates. Your relationship with your cards is personal and should be determined by your beliefs and what works for you.

There are two schools of thought regarding letting other people touch your cards. Some people prefer to have no one else touch their cards because they do not want anyone else's energy to influence the cards. Other people believe that the querent must touch the cards, usually by shuffling, in order to get an accurate reading. Sometimes after someone else has handled the cards, people will put the cards back in order as a way of cleansing the deck and getting it ready for the next reading.

Some people cleanse their decks regularly, especially if they have done a number of readings, or sporadically, perhaps after they've done a reading that dealt with a deeply troubling issue. Cleansing can be done, as mentioned above, by putting the cards in order. Or you can pass the cards through the smoke of burning sage, store the deck with a stone or crystal with cleansing properties (such a rose quartz), or let the cards sit in the light of a full moon (inside on a window ledge, not outside!).

In addition to cleansing, some people believe that silk cloth and oak have protective qualities and that's why they store their cards in these materials. Other people store their cards with gems, crystals, or herbs that impart qualities they seek as a reader, such as healing, clarity of vision, wisdom, etc. At the very least, you'll want to keep your cards in a box or pouch to make sure all the cards stay together and none are lost. Some people decorate the box or pouch with symbols or runes that represent wisdom, discernment, the ability to communicate, etc.

Care and storage of your cards is a combination of personal beliefs and practicality. Try different methods until you find the ones that are most comfortable and effective for you.

Divination

Divination, fortunetelling, knowing the future—what heady and beguiling notions! But unless you believe that the future is set in stone, that everything is predetermined, and that you have no free will, the future cannot be predicted, right? Well, yes and no. If certain events are set in motion, then there is a likely outcome. Think about predicting the weather. The further out a prediction, the more likely things will happen to change the forecast. The daily forecast is always more accurate than the seven-day forecast. Even with the daily forecast, unforeseen events can change the weather very quickly.

A tarot reading, or divination, is most effective if used like a weather forecast. It can tell you what will probably happen if all things remain as they are and give you a clear picture of all the elements involved and how they affect one another. But unlike a weather forecast, the tarot can also help you determine your best course of action in those events over which you have control. Because the tarot acts as a bridge between your subconscious and your conscious, it can help clarify your thoughts and feelings regarding a situation. The tarot is also a spiritual tool, serving as a connection between you and the divine—it can provide guidance in times of turmoil. In short, it can give you information about a situation and help you find answers or make better decisions.

Asking the Question

Searching for answers or information is not always easy. An Internet search using the wrong keyword generally ends in frustration. Not asking for specific directions can get us somewhere other than where we intended to go. We can make things easier for ourselves by realizing that getting the best, most useful answer depends largely on asking the best question.

Working with the idea that the future is not predestined, phrasing the question gains more importance than even the desire to efficiently access information. Careful construction of the question is the first step in a useful tarot reading. Sometimes the act of examining the phrasing will tell you as much about the situation and yourself as the tarot reading itself. Imagine you are dating someone named Matt. The answers to the questions "Will I marry Matt?" or "Should I marry Matt?" really do not provide any insight. Instead, consider why you are asking these questions. Do you want to marry Matt? Why? If you are unsure, what are the issues that disturb you? Do you think that Matt doesn't want to marry you? Why?

Consider why you are even approaching the tarot about your relationship with Matt. What are your doubts and concerns? Do you have a clear sense of your goal in the relationship? If so, do you see roadblocks? In short, you need to be very clear on what it is you want to know and why. Once you have reflected on the situation, you can construct a question to meet your needs. Let's say Matt is interested in marriage to you, but you are not certain you want to and are not sure why. There is a nagging doubt that you cannot identify. A possible question could be "What is the root of my uncertainty about marriage with Matt?" The answer to that question could perhaps lead to another question. Once the issue is identified, you could explore possible solutions to or actions in response to your newfound knowledge.

Let's change the scenario. In this one, you are certain that you want to marry Matt. Matt, however, has his doubts. He cannot or does not choose to discuss them. What can you do? Many readers consider it unethical to read for or about other people directly without their consent. If Matt consents, then the two of you could form a question and consult the deck together. If not, then you must think more about what you want in the situation as it stands. If Matt is unwilling to commit, do you wish to stay in the relationship? If you are unsure, you could ask the cards "What are the pros and cons of staying in this relationship?" Or you might ask what you can do to facilitate more open communication between the two of you.

Sometimes you won't have a specific question. Occasionally people feel a vague sense of disconnection, of imbalance. Everything may seem okay, but underneath the surface there is something missing. Just as there are times when you may meditate or pray just to enjoy the sense of peace, to listen to the quiet voice that sometimes attends your spirit, there are times when the tarot has something to communicate. During these times, when analysis fails and yet your intuition feels like it is hitting you over the head with a baseball bat, it is best to simply ask the cards "What do I need to know right now?"

Exercise 5

𝒲rite down a question you'd like answered. Don't analyze the question yet, just write it as it pops into your mind. Is it worded in a way that empowers you or in a way that makes you feel like a victim of circumstance? Reword the question in different ways. Try clarifying what you want to happen or asking for actions you can take to achieve your desired outcome.

Once you have formed your question, you will need to select a spread for your reading. While the question forms the foundation for the answer, the spread forms the framework or the shape for that answer. Understanding the spread's role in a reading and selecting the right one are just as important as understanding and phrasing your question.

The Basics

◆

21

What Is a Tarot Spread?

Most people are familiar with the scenario of shuffling the cards and laying them out in some sort of pattern (called a spread or a layout). This ordering of the cards provides a framework for the wisdom of the tarot to emerge and for the reader to form an answer. Each position represents a different aspect of the question, such as "the card that comes up in this position represents you" or "the card that comes up here indicates the possible outcome." Here is the first choice: do you use a spread that is already created, such as the standard Celtic Cross (one of the most popular spreads), or design your own spread—or use a combination of the two?

Using an already created spread has advantages, especially for beginners who may feel they are learning too much at one time. If that is the case, by all means use a predesigned spread. Just be aware of the limitations. There are books of spreads available (for example, *How to Use Tarot Spreads* by Sylvia Abraham). At the end of this book, you'll also find a collection of spreads that may be useful to you. You can look through them and pick one that most closely matches the needs posed by your question. If you are interested in creating your own spreads, feel free to experiment on your own, using the question to direct the shape of the spread or modifying an existing spread to more accurately reflect your question. For further information, consult *Designing Your Own Tarot Spreads* by Teresa Michelsen.

Significticators

In some spreads, such as the Celtic Cross, there is a position for a significator card. This is simply a card that represents the querent. It is used as a focus point but is not usually incorporated into the reading, although there are two instances when it can be beneficial to include it, which will be discussed later.

Traditionally, a significator is selected through one of four ways:

• Simply use the Magician to represent a male querent or the High Priestess to represent a female querent.

• Select a court card to represent the querent based on physical coloring and age, using the lists below.

• Select a court card based on astrological sign and age, using the lists below.

• Select a court card based on personality and age, using the lists below.

Physical Appearance

WANDS: Fair skin with blond hair and blue eyes.

CUPS: Light to medium skin with light-brown hair and blue or hazel eyes.

SWORDS: Olive skin with dark hair and light eyes.

PENTACLES: Dark skin with dark hair and dark eyes.

Astrological Sign

WANDS: Aries, Leo, Sagittarius (fire signs).

CUPS: Cancer, Scorpio, Pisces (water signs).

SWORDS: Gemini, Libra, Aquarius (air signs).

PENTACLES: Taurus, Virgo, Capricorn (earth signs).

Personality

WANDS: A fiery, passionate, energetic person.

CUPS: An emotional, creative person.

SWORDS: An intellectual, logical person.

PENTACLES: A down-to-earth, practical person.

Age

PAGE: A child or young woman.

KNIGHT: A young man.

QUEEN: A mature woman.

KING: A mature man.

These methods have definite limitations. First and foremost, it takes that card out of the deck so that it cannot come up in the reading itself. This is particularly unfortunate in the case of using the Magician or High Priestess—two very important Major Arcana cards. Selecting a court card can also be problematic.

In the case of physical description, not all possible combinations are accounted for. If you use the fourth method, what person is completely logical or emotional? The court cards usually represent one facet of a personality, so to pick one to represent a whole person is an oversimplification. On the other hand, you can select how the person feels in relation to the question. For example, if they are normally a very rational person but feel overly emotional in the situation in question, you could select a Cup rather than a Sword.

Two other ways of selecting significators have gained in popularity and can actually be useful in terms of the reading itself. The first is to let the deck select the card. That is, shuffle the cards and use the top card for the significator. In this method, the significator can show how the querent feels or the role she or he plays in the situation. In addition, it can be read as another facet of the second card in the Celtic Cross, which also represents the querent. (See page 146 for the Celtic Cross spread.)

A second method works well with someone who is unfamiliar with the cards. Let the querent go through the whole deck and pick a card that she or he thinks represents her- or himself. This can provide interesting insight into how the person sees her- or himself in the situation and can be read in conjunction with card eight in the Celtic Cross, which represents how the querent sees her- or himself.

Play with the various methods and see what works for you. You may wish to disregard significators altogether or you may even develop your own method of selecting them.

Exercise 6

  $\mathcal{P}$ick a significator for yourself using each of the methods described above. Compare the cards that you came up with in each instance. Which one seems most accurate? Why? Try selecting significators for other people you know. See if one method gives consistently more accurate results.

Reversals

Just as some readers use significators and some do not, some people read reversed cards. Reversed cards are cards that show up in the spread upside down. Some people believe that the seventy-eight cards of the tarot already represent a full range of human experience and reversals just muddy the waters. New students of tarot often feel intimidated by learning yet another set of seventy-eight meanings. Others argue that using reversals adds depth, subtlety, and accuracy to a reading, and that reversals are a way of fine-tuning your interpretations.

Like significators, this is a decision you must make for yourself. If you choose not to read reversals and cards appear upside down in your spread, simply turn them right-side up. Many seasoned tarot readers recommend that you first become comfortable with the cards upright before attempting reversed meanings. If you want to include reversed meanings in your readings, then you need to make another decision: how are you going to interpret reversals? You'll want to use a coherent theory determining the reversed meanings. If you decide on a specific method, one that simply modifies the upright meaning, your job is much easier because you won't be learning seventy-eight new meanings. You'll simply be modifying the upright meanings in some way.

Tarot experts offer many different practices for interpreting reversed cards. The most comprehensive work on this subject is Mary K. Greer's *Complete Book of Tarot Reversals*. If you are at all interested in reversals, this book is highly recommended. For the moment, though, let's examine some simple possibilities to experiment with. The first and most obvious method is to say that the reversed card means the exact opposite of the upright meaning. Another method is to say the energy represented by the upright card is blocked or may be delayed in some way. A method that many readers find useful is to say that the reversed card is the same as the upright card but, by turning up reversed, the card is indicating that special attention should be paid to it. Another option is to use the negative, extreme aspect of each card's meaning (see page 35).

Try different methods and see which one works for you. Once you've settled on a practice, stay consistent.

Exercise 7

*S*elect three cards that you feel comfortable with. Try interpreting them as reversals in each of the methods described. Which method felt right to you? Why?

Performing a Reading

Once you've formed your question, selected your spread, and made your decisions about significators and reversals, and have some level of confidence about how to interpret the cards, you are ready to start doing readings. You will need to mix the cards by shuffling any way that is comfortable for you or laying them on the table and mixing them like you're making mud pies or playing in finger paint. Focus on your question as you mix the cards. When you are ready, put the cards in a neat pile and either lay the cards out one by one from the top of the deck or fan them out facedown and select each card.

Lay out each card in the order indicated by the spread. You can lay them facedown so that all you see are the backs of the cards, or faceup so that you see what all the cards are right away. There are benefits to both methods. If they are facedown and you flip them over one at a time, it increases the sense of mystery and excitement and also allows you to more easily focus on each card as it is revealed. By laying the cards faceup, you get an opportunity to see the spread as a whole before beginning to read each card. This can be helpful in determining the theme of the answer. For example, many Major Arcana cards might indicate a very spiritual focus; many Cups could show a very emotional situation; several aces may indicate a time of beginnings. Sometimes symbols or colors can speak to the answer as well. If you see a lot of red, it could indicate a fiery, passionate, or volatile situation.

Once you've laid out the cards, begin interpreting them, keeping in mind what position each card is in, as that affects the interpretation. Once you've finished, you might want to record your reading in a journal or notebook. This is highly recommended. By doing this, you can see if certain cards keep appearing in your readings. Also, you can go back to your readings and check your accuracy of interpreting the spread and your objectivity. Hindsight is always twenty-twenty. Even if your objectivity isn't all that you'd hoped for at the moment, you can develop it. By reviewing your readings and seeing how what you wanted affected your interpretation, you'll be better prepared to guard against that in the future.

By recording your readings, you will also see how your skills change and improve. Doing a reading isn't difficult, but it does take practice. Not only do you need to know the card meanings, you need to weave the cards in the spread together, taking into account their positions in the spread, to form a coherent story.

Exercise 8

*B*efore doing a reading, try this exercise as a warmup. We'll use a common three-card spread, where all three cards are laid out in a horizontal line. The first card represents the past, the middle card the present, and the last card the future. In this exercise, though, we'll have the positions represent the beginning, the middle, and the end of a story. Shuffle your cards and lay out three. Make up a story using the three cards in order. Doing this exercise will help you flow the cards together into a whole instead of seeing them as unconnected parts.

The Finishing Touches

So now you have the tools you need to perform divinations. Maybe the process isn't as theatrical or mysterious as you expected. Maybe you wanted a little more drama. Although little extras certainly aren't necessary, they don't hurt. In fact, they can be helpful. Rituals, simple or elaborate, help focus the mind and can provide useful, positive energy. Here are just a few ideas you might want to experiment with:

- Create a space for your reading by setting the mood. Burn candles and/or incense selected to promote concentration, communication, or union with the divine. Have physical representations of the suits nearby as a reminder to seek balance in your readings: a candle or twig for Wands (Fire); a chalice or glass of water for Cups (Water); a small knife, feather, or incense for Swords (Air); and a stone or bit of soil for Pentacles (Earth).

- Prepare yourself by centering and grounding yourself. Take a few deep breaths, pray, or meditate before or while shuffling.

- Create a ritual for shuffling your deck. Many readers choose to shuffle seven times, both because seven is a mystical number and because it randomizes the deck very well. Some people like to cut the deck in three piles and then gather them up in random order before dealing the cards.

- At the end of the reading, store your deck for the next time, cleansing it or storing it with stones, crystals, or herbs, if you choose. If you wrap your deck in a large enough cloth, you can use the cloth on the table to lay your cards on. One hint here: don't select a busy or overly colorful cloth, as it might compete visually with the images on the cards. The images on the cards should be your main focus.

THE
Major Arcana

*T*he images and meanings in each Tarot card are complex and sometimes contradictory. They cover a range of meanings, from extreme to extreme. For example, a mother can care for and nurture her children, and we see that as positive. However, if the mother's attention is too possessive or obsessive, the nurturing can turn to smothering or control. For each card, you'll read a description and general meaning followed by dangerous extremes that are also part of the card's meaning.

Exercise 9

*A*s you read about each card, look at the image. Write down what speaks to you and note what does not. Compare these observations to the notes you made in Exercise 3. How are they similar and how do they differ? Make note of an experience in your life that relates to each card.

_____

_____

_____

_____

_____

_____

_____

_____

_____

_____

_____

_____

_____

The Major Arcana

◆

0, The Fool

$\mathcal{T}$he Fool is at the beginning of his journey. All possibilities and seeming contradictions exist in this moment. The signs of the zodiac that he so carelessly juggles indicate both the science of the heavens and the vastness of human imagination. These symbols represent all types of personality traits. Which one will he end up with? Will he make this important choice or will the choice be made for him by chance? Is he playing when he should be serious, or is his play filled with wisdom? Speaking of playing, is that gold hoop at his feet something he should be paying attention to, or is it a possible distraction? The Fool does not know, nor does he much care. He lives in the moment, filled with wonder and curiosity, not worried about where the journey will end.

The Fool's message is one of unconventional choices. Take a leap of faith. Adopt a playful attitude in a serious situation. You are at a crossroads and you have no way of knowing where each road will end. Pick one that strikes your fancy and set out with courage and a light heart. Prepare to meet all challenges with confidence.

Be aware of carelessness and folly. There is a difference between taking a risk and plowing headfirst into danger. Reckless behavior can lead to a long path of unhappiness.

_____

_____

_____

_____

_____

_____

_____

_____

_____

_____

_____

_____

_____

The Major Arcana

◆

I, The Magician

$\mathcal{T}$he Magician is a serious man at a serious business. A master magic-maker, the Magician is also something of a man of science. Unlike the Fool, he is fully aware of the laws of cause and effect, actions and consequences. He is aware of the power of his will. He is aware of the importance of his choices. By focusing his will, he controls the elemental powers represented by the Wand, Cup, Sword, and Pentacle, which are his tools. By learning to control his will and the elements, he can accomplish whatever he chooses.

The Magician's message is one of discipline and responsibility. You have the power within yourself to accomplish whatever you wish. You have the necessary tools at your disposal. Focus your will and hone your skills.

Be aware of control and manipulation. Power can blind you to what is appropriate. Keep in mind the negative stereotype of the Magician as a charlatan or a swindler.

_____

_____

_____

_____

_____

_____

_____

_____

_____

_____

_____

_____

The Major Arcana

♦

II, The High Priestess

$\mathcal{T}$he High Priestess speaks of the unknown and contradictions. While her face is masked, she is clothed with a transparent gown. She floats with a toe barely skimming the waters of the subconscious while her head is crowned with nine glowing orbs representing the nine planets. She exists between two pillars holding mechanisms whose purpose is unclear. The night sky behind her hints at both the poetic mystery of the moon and the logically charted courses of the heavenly bodies. She beguiles, she promises knowledge; she can be dangerous. We must accept her energy and wisdom cautiously.

The message of the High Priestess is about a kind of knowing that is beyond logic. Pay attention to your intuition and recognize that there are different ways of knowing. While the stars and planets of the night sky can be charted and understood rationally, this same sky inspires us in ways foreign to our sense of reason.

Be aware of staying too long in the heady realms of the High Priestess. You must take your inspiration and translate it into action. Honor the muse, but do not become her slave.

The Major Arcana

♦

III, The Empress

$\mathcal{T}$he Empress follows the High Priestess just as inspiration is ideally followed by manifestation. Circled by astrological symbols representing the possibilities of life, her red belt and her fiery hair speak of earthly passion and sensuality. Covering her passion, though, is her blue, flowing cloak, representing emotion. A solar system-like necklace hangs near her heart. Her action is largely internal and nurturing, surrounded with feeling. She is the Mother archetype from whom all life flows. She holds a circle with a cross, a symbol of the feminine and also a symbol of the balance of opposites—both the idea and the physical form of the idea. At the most basic level, she is both the epitome of love and the birth of a life resulting from that love.

The message of the Empress is that of creation and passion. You are in a position to nurture and give birth to a project. Tap into the energy of Mother Earth and celebrate her gifts. Recognize, honor, and celebrate your senses, the physical world, and nature.

Be aware of maintaining a healthy balance. Do not let your emotions or actions become obsessive or controlling, and do not allow a chaotic proliferation by trying to do too much. A garden needs careful and loving cultivation—too much or too little upsets the delicate balance of beauty.

_____

_____

_____

_____

_____

_____

_____

_____

_____

_____

_____

_____

IV, The Emperor

*I*n many ways the Emperor is the mirror image of the Empress. Perhaps most obvious is the reversal of their clothing's color. The passionate red of the Emperor's garment is external, as are his actions. He is surrounded not by the abstract glyph symbols of the Empress but by more realistic signs of the zodiac. He holds his representation of the solar system in his hand, showing a more external control than the Empress. While driven by love and a desire for what is best for everyone, as indicated by his blue undercloak, he is more concerned with the realistic functioning of everyday life. On a social level, he seeks to create stability so that society can reach its highest good. As a Father archetype, he wishes to give his children a strong foundation, allowing them to achieve their best.

The message of the Emperor is that of healthy stability. Create an environment that allows you to function at your best. Seek well-functioning order in your life in terms of your home, your workplace, and your relationships. Appreciate the rules of society that allow a smooth and peaceful life.

Be aware of stifling and stagnating rules and regulations. Creating order in your life simply for the sake of order alone is inhibiting, not liberating. Learn when it is time to question the obligations and mores of society.

_____

_____

_____

_____

_____

_____

_____

_____

_____

_____

_____

_____

V, The Hierophant

A leader and teacher wearing vestments, indicating wisdom, almost fades into the background. The stained glass window enveloping him brings to mind the great cathedrals of the past, incredible poems of glass and stone reaching toward heaven. This is an apt symbol of humankind's greatest achievements of understanding the physical and spiritual worlds. A view of the universe—of all that there is to know, both physically and spiritually—lies beyond. Looking at these elements as three levels, we see in the background the knowable universe, then humankind's understanding and utilization of this knowledge, and finally the passing on of that knowledge to individual people through formal education and religious training.

The message of the Hierophant reminds us of the marvelous accomplishments of humankind and of the great resources of knowledge that are available to us. Respect the achievements of generations past. Use that knowledge to create with usefulness and beauty. Do not disdain tradition out of hand but see what wonderful things it has to offer.

Be aware of following tradition blindly. Do not accept all knowledge without question; rather, question authority. Make sure all beliefs and practices make sense to your own heart and mind before you make them part of your life.

_____

_____

_____

_____

_____

_____

_____

_____

_____

_____

_____

_____

The Major Arcana

◆

VI, The Lovers

A perfect, passionate union rises, romantic and idealized, from the waters of our subconscious and our dreams. More than romance, more than a man and a woman, we see here the elements necessary to achieve such a union. The couple is grounded in water, showing a deep connection of their emotions. The warrior's red clothing and the deep orange of the sunset surround the scene with fiery passion. The beauty and abandon of the woman suggests earthly sensuality. The dolphins, although creatures of water, indicate intelligence and communication that are characteristic of the element of air. Finally, the upward motion of the couple and woman's gaze toward the heavens illustrate a higher focus on the spiritual realm.

The message of the Lovers tells us to make good and balanced choices. Indeed, the original meaning of this card in the earliest Tarot decks was called the Choice and showed a man choosing between two women. Consider all the facets before committing to any decision. Choose well and build a foundation that can help you achieve your best dreams.

Be aware of letting one element of a choice overshadow all else. A relationship with simply a physical attraction, a career decision with only an intellectual appeal, or a home opportunity with decadent amenities may not be the best choice in the long run.

_____

_____

_____

_____

_____

_____

_____

_____

_____

_____

_____

_____

VII, The Chariot

The Chariot is a card of victory. The medallion of the sun atop the chariot indicates the immense power and focus of the woman's mind. Although victory seems a rather straightforward concept, the card is full of contradictions. A woman in royal purple rides in a chariot. Instead of horses and forward movement, we see two sphinxes. Sphinxes often symbolize riddles. Their silver and gold color represents opposing ideas. The woman appears to be driving this motionless vehicle without reins; indeed, she is looking off in another direction. Yes, this is a card of victory. She has control, gained perhaps by strength of will alone. But she has not resolved the riddle of opposing ideas. She has achievement but not understanding.

The message of the Chariot is one of willpower and control. Recognize your own strength and ability to maintain order in the midst of chaos. Know that you can achieve more than you think you can. Celebrate your accomplishments.

Be aware of repressing issues or turning away from ideas that puzzle you. Once you achieve your goals, do not come to a complete stop, thinking that you have arrived. There is always more to learn and accomplish.

_____

_____

_____

_____

_____

_____

_____

_____

_____

_____

_____

_____

_____

VIII, Strength

A woman with a great sense of purpose walks side by side with a lion. There is a chain wrapped loosely around the lion's neck and held just as loosely in the woman's hand. The lion is the woman's animal instincts. These instincts neither lead her nor are they dragged along behind her. They are there, a reserve of strength, power, and courage, for whenever she should have need of them.

The message of Strength reminds you that you have more strength, power, and courage than you realize. Learn to live easily with these gifts and use them when appropriate.

Be aware of two extremes. Do not let your strength or baser desires control you. Conversely, do not deny your own power.

_____

_____

_____

_____

_____

_____

_____

_____

_____

_____

_____

_____

_____

IX, The Hermit

A mysterious old man walks a lonely, narrow path. He carries a light, representing his mind and the knowledge he has acquired, and a staff, symbolizing the power of his will. His red belt indicates something of the passion that drives him in his search. While he has much knowledge of the world and a strong will, there is still much that is unresolved in his heart. Alone, he goes off to contemplate, to compare conventional knowledge to what he feels in his heart.

The message of the Hermit is one of self-knowledge. It is time for you to withdraw, contemplate what you know, and make sure your beliefs reflect the leading of your own heart. Now you must learn who you are and what you believe. Then you can trust yourself without depending on the opinions of others.

Be aware of withdrawing too long or for the wrong reasons. Withdrawing from life out of fear or to avoid personal responsibility is not the same as self-examination.

_____

_____

_____

_____

_____

_____

_____

_____

_____

_____

_____

_____

_____

_____

The Major Arcana

◆

X, Wheel of Fortune

*S*ometimes viewed as Fate, this wheel frightens most of us because its turning is beyond our control. Here we have a fully mechanized wheel that is, as indicated by the astrological symbols on it, controlled by the stars, the rhythms of nature and life. Sometimes things happen in our lives that seem inexplicable, but life is full of cycles and we would do well to remember that. The sun at the center of the wheel can represent our mind. If we are centered and secure, then no matter how the wheel turns, we are not at its mercy. We can view something however we like—as a blessing or curse, a tragedy or an opportunity.

The message of the Wheel of Fortune is twofold. First, know that life has ups and downs and many times things happen that affect you but are not, strictly speaking, personal. For example, the company you work for is bought by another and restructured. Your job is eliminated. This was not done to hurt you personally, although it does affect you deeply. Second, events in life are often good or bad simply because you choose to view them as such. Keep your center and your focus and don't be rattled by events you cannot control.

Be aware of using the cycles of the wheel to neglect personal responsibility. Keep in mind the things that are within your control and do not blame circumstances for mistakes that are truly your own.

_____

_____

_____

_____

_____

_____

_____

_____

_____

_____

_____

_____

_____

The Major Arcana

◆

XI, Justice

The personification of Justice stands with the past and future held in her hands. The scales represent the karmic balance of life that must be maintained. The image of the sun is you, directly in the middle of your past and your future. Justice is blindfolded; she has no power to help or hurt you. You have made your own karma. Whatever you have done in the past will determine your future.

The message of Justice is simple. You make your own future by your actions. You are at a point where you are questioning why something is happening. Look to your past actions. How have they created the current situation? This is a time for taking responsibility for your life.

Be aware of giving way to despondency. While past mistakes have future ramifications, your present actions will also shape the future. Learn from your mistakes and make choices now that lead to a happier future.

_____

_____

_____

_____

_____

_____

_____

_____

_____

_____

_____

_____

_____

The Major Arcana

◆

XII, The Hanging Man

*M*ore than any other figure in the Major Arcana, the Hanging Man resembles the Fool. By turning himself upside down, by behaving in a manner not consistent with society, the Hanging Man may be judged a fool by many. The difference between the two is important, though. The Hanging Man has come through a challenging experience that gives him a sense of peace and understanding that only people who've successfully faced great trials can have. The sun represents his vision of himself and his place in the universe. He may flounder at times, but he knows who he is and from whence he gets his strength. He is willing to sacrifice society's approval in order to be true to himself.

The message of the Hanging Man is knowing when and what to sacrifice. Be clear about who you are and let all your actions and decisions hang from that vision. Even if your actions feel clumsy or out of sync with others, sacrifice their favorable opinion rather than be untrue to yourself. Do not put more stock in what other people think than in what you believe to be right.

Be aware of rationalizing bizarre or inappropriate behavior by saying you are just being yourself. Are you really? Or are you looking for an excuse to misbehave while feeling noble about it?

_____

_____

_____

_____

_____

_____

_____

_____

_____

_____

_____

_____

XIII, Death

*E*veryone faces death in some guise. Here, we are speaking of a psychological death rather than a physical death. In this card, the skull stares with inexorable resolve. The chilling message is: If you want to move past this point, you have to pass through death. Why would anyone want to; what is the incentive? Death holds the rewards on his banner and shield. The white flower symbolizes a purity of desire, and the white horse a purity of will. Anyone wanting to continue on their spiritual journey needs these. They indicate the death of the ego and with it long-held beliefs that are no longer useful. This must happen to make way for new energy and life.

The message of Death is that spiritual growth brings pain. It isn't easy to let go of certain behaviors or beliefs, to admit errors in thought and practice. Without negating the magnitude of ego-death, the emblems of what is to come—greater spiritual strength—remind us that the endeavor is not without its reward.

Be aware of the fear of change, of letting go of outmoded ideas. Fear of change leads to stagnation, which might be longer lasting and more painful than a clean death.

XIV, Temperance

 A fiery woman, full of passion and spark, is perhaps an incongruent image for a card meaning moderation. Like the gold and silver sphinxes in the chariot, the gold and silver cups represent extremes. Temperance means to mix or to blend, as this woman is tempering extremes—any extremes—in behavior, belief, or feeling. She has learned to temper her life in such a way that she maintains and expresses her passion perfectly. By learning to do this, she is living her life as fully as possible, with her internal beliefs in perfect harmony with her external actions and with the world around her.

The message of Temperance is simple to understand yet difficult to practice. Moderate your life in all ways: physically, spiritually, emotionally, and intellectually. Let your action (or inaction) be appropriate to the situation. This card, more than any other in the tarot, speaks of perfect balance perfectly expressed.

Be aware of intemperance and extremes in behavior. Also, don't let the fear of making a mistake lead you to constant inaction. While inaction is sometimes the right choice, it is not always.

_____

_____

_____

_____

_____

_____

_____

_____

_____

_____

_____

_____

_____

The Major Arcana

XV, The Devil

Intriguing, powerful, compelling; what a dangerous and attractive figure this is. The mask, while adding to the mysterious allure, warns us that this man is hiding something. He wears a pentacle, giving a hint of his earthiness and sensual pleasures. However, because his eyes are blinded, he pursues these pleasures blindly, without consideration for anything else. He is obsession, bondage, and destructive practices. He is what happens—what we can become—when our lives go very badly out of balance.

The message of the Devil is a warning, a cautionary tale. If Temperance is perfect balance perfectly expressed, the Devil is imperfect balance recklessly pursued. Anything in the extreme—eating, working, sexual activity, exercising—leads to an unbalanced life. Take heed and moderate your behavior. Keep watch for obsessions in your life. Do not let any belief or practice overshadow all other aspects of your life or your responsibilities to yourself and others.

Be aware of being so afraid of pleasures out of fear of addiction that you repress or deny all desires, even healthy ones.

_____

_____

_____

_____

_____

_____

_____

_____

_____

_____

_____

_____

_____

The Major Arcana

◆

XVI, The Tower

$\mathcal{C}$arefully crafted, tall, beautiful, and strong, the Tower represents our worldview. We have added to it and altered it as needed. We expected it to last and serve us well. It is hit by lightning, a literal bolt from the blue, and is destroyed. The bolt symbolizes, in some form or another, a moment of illumination, of realization, of experience, that shakes our world to its very foundation. We fall, like the naked man, from the structure. We have to rebuild. And we have nothing . . . or so it seems. However, don't discount what the flash of lightning reveals to you.

The message of the Tower is a difficult one. Unlike the Wheel, with its philosophical message of centeredness, and Death, with its promise of spiritual enlightenment, the Tower doesn't seem to offer much except destruction. Our belief system helps us find calm in the center of the Wheel and gives us courage to face Death. In the Tower that belief system is shattered. The good news is that it is usually shattered by a truth that we didn't recognize before. Knowing the truth is good; ignorance is not really bliss.

Be aware of overdramatizing situations. If you overreact to every upset in your life, you may find yourself ill prepared to deal with real trauma or tragedy.

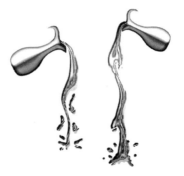

_____

_____

_____

_____

_____

_____

_____

_____

_____

_____

_____

_____

The Major Arcana

◆

XVII, The Star

*E*verything here speaks of peace, calm, and hope. This woman represents perfect faith. The star on her forehead is connected with the star in the sky, showing a unity of thought and spirit. This woman knows that the mechanisms of the heavens are working perfectly and that everything happens in its proper time. Sister to Temperance, the Star is more natural in her nakedness, more grounded in her humble position in the water. Rather than controlling and conserving liquid, like her sister, she unreservedly empties her pitchers, having faith that they will be filled again.

The message of the Star is replenishment and faith. Know that the cycles of nature are true and natural and that after a hard time, a better time will follow. And when it comes, give yourself over to it—immerse yourself in the cool waters of faith and the constant light of the Star. Know that your heart will be refreshed and your faith will be renewed.

Be aware of lack of faith, of giving in to despair, of giving up. The Star promises hope. Don't lose faith in that promise.

_____

_____

_____

_____

_____

_____

_____

_____

_____

_____

_____

_____

XVIII, The Moon

*T*his beautiful orb inspires us like no other. It speaks to our soul. It releases our animal instincts, like the dogs howling. It invites the crayfish to surface—this alien creature represents our deepest fears. The light of the Moon allows us to glimpse it, but provides enough shadow that we can ignore it if we're careful. The moon goddess heightens our intuition. She does show us our worst nightmares . . . but then again, she gives us our best dreams as well.

The message of the Moon is as shadowy as a moonlit night. Pay attention to your dreams and your intuition. Face your fears, even if you do so a little at a time. Attend to your soul.

Be aware of not seeing clearly, of being afraid of shadows, or of being led astray by shadowy images that aren't what they seem.

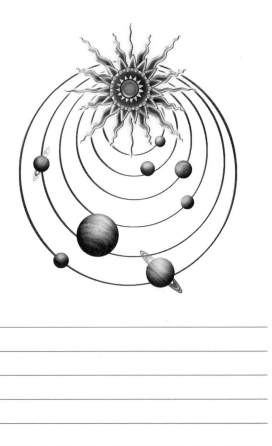

_____

_____

_____

_____

_____

_____

_____

_____

_____

_____

_____

_____

_____

The Major Arcana

◆

XIX, The Sun

$\mathscr{T}$he sun, the planets, the stars of the zodiac—everything is clear and in good working order. Not only that, but you can see the order. You see the scientific charting of the heavenly courses. You see the astrological symbols and know that the cold, mathematically knowable sky is more than that—that myths and stories abound even there. You see the universe with its layers of meanings and contradictions and you are at ease with it.

The message of the Sun is that of peaceful contentment with the world and its workings. You understand what you can and don't fret about what you don't. You understand yourself and your role in the universe as much as you can, and you are okay with that, too. Life doesn't get much better than this.

Be aware that you may not be used to such ease and happiness. Be careful not to fight it. Enjoy it as much as you can. Oh, and don't try to analyze it too much.

_____

_____

_____

_____

_____

_____

_____

_____

_____

_____

_____

_____

_____

XX, Judgement

*A*n angel wears a winged helmet, bringing to mind Mercury, the planet governing communication. Underlining the idea of communication, the angel sounds a horn, calling people from their former lives to new ones. They are being called to judge for themselves their old lives and compare them to their new ones. They will decide for themselves whether or not they answer the call.

The message of Judgement is clear. You are being called to do something. You might not want to hear it and are actively drowning it out with noise of your daily life. You might be afraid of the call and the changes it will bring. Listen to it and face it with courage and action. It promises a more fulfilling life.

Be aware of two things: First, of ignoring the call or shirking from it in fear or obstinance; second, of mistaking the desires of others or of society for a true calling. Do not feel compelled to dance to anyone else's tune, and do not ignore the music of your own heart.

_____
_____
_____
_____
_____
_____
_____
_____
_____
_____
_____
_____
_____
_____
_____

The Major Arcana

◆

XXI, The World

A woman stands with poise, dignity, and assurance. She stands before the world surrounded by laurel wreaths, indicating her mastery. She holds wands, representing her will, in both hands. Unlike the other figures in the Major Arcana, her will is in tune with both sides of herself; she has achieved balance of her consciousness and unconsciousness. She celebrates a great accomplishment. For this, she is recognized by the world and, more importantly, by her own self.

The message of the World is that of completion and accomplishment. You feel a sense of unity with the universe and mastery over self that is natural and effortless. You move to the rhythm of nature and of your heart. They are one.

Be aware of a false sense of security. In theory, the World represents total completion. However, in our human lives, this is never really achieved. But because we are human still, we can achieve only partial or temporary oneness. These temporary or partial experiences encourage us to keep growing and moving forward, if for no other reason than to experience that exquisite moment of freedom and understanding again.

THE
Minor Arcana

*W*hile the Major Arcana are archetypal energies, the Minor Arcana are the echoes of those energies in daily life. They are the experiences that make up our existence. Each Minor Arcana describes a situation and sometimes offers advice that harkens back to the Major Arcana of the same number.

Exercise 10

*A*s we learned, the numbers on the Minor Arcana have meanings. Take the four aces and compare how each suit expresses the meaning of "one." Do this for two, three, four, and so on. Notice how the suit affects and shapes the number's meaning.

Wands

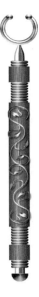

Ace of Wands

$\mathcal{L}$ike all of the aces, this is a gift from the universe. Unlike the other aces, the Ace of Wands is bestowed by human hands, indicating a facet of the universe more sympathetic to the human condition. In some ways this is the kindest, most generous gift of the aces. It is the beginning of everything—the spark of life. It is also the gift of will, of inspiration, of action, of passion, of courage. This illumination from the heavens is the start of all our ideas and projects. Like the Magician, Major Arcana I, it is about a connection to higher planes, a focus of will, and the ability to achieve goals.

You are at a propitious point. You are given a gift, an idea, a project, or career opportunity. Take advantage of it with confidence and gratitude.

Be aware of ignoring opportunities and inaction. The Ace of Wands is a gift that requires the recipient to take action.

Two of Wands

$\mathcal{A}$ traveler faces a fork in the road and a difficult decision. Outwardly, this card is reminiscent of the Fool. Unlike the Fool, he is conscious of the future and wants to make the best choice—not an easy task when the choices are so similar. The differences lie far off on the horizon. Which is better, the bright sky and huge mountain or the red sky and smaller mountain? And what of the deer? Standing like guardians, what will they do after the traveler selects? How will his choice immediately change the situation? Like the High Priestess, Major Arcana II, the traveler must tap into a deeper level of knowing.

You are at a crossroads. The correct choice is unclear, at least in terms of logic, because there are too many unknowns. The Wands are not about logic; they are about inspiration and courage. Follow your gut and move ahead bravely.

Be aware of stagnation. The Wands are about action. This is not a time to stand still.

Three of Wands

A man stands on the shore watching a ship sail off. Or perhaps it is returning. Either way, he has invested in it. Whether he sees success or failure, his future is for the moment out of his control. He cannot affect its outcome. This is probably the most difficult card of the Wands. Like the Empress, Major Arcana III, this is a time of gestation, not of action or control.

You have made a choice and now must wait for the results. Whether you are patient or impatient doesn't really matter—it will not affect the outcome. It is, though, a good opportunity to learn patience and self-control.

Be aware of agitated action. Although it is frustrating to be still, let things take their course. Do not work yourself up needlessly.

Four of Wands

$\mathscr{A}$ contented, affectionate family stands amongst four wands topped with a wreath of flowers. They have focused their will and achieved a stable, satisfying result. The rabbits indicate a time of abundance. The dragonfly shows an overlying sense of happiness. The wreath represents a sense of unity and beauty. Like the Emperor, Major Arcana IV, they worked together for the good of all and created an environment where they can all find fulfillment.

You have achieved a satisfying goal. Take time to celebrate this. Be proud of what you have done.

Be aware of dissatisfaction. This is not the time to be critical of your accomplishment.

Five of Wands

$\mathscr{I}$n a clearing, five men compete. They use their wands, representing their wills and abilities, to spar. By doing so, they learn their own strengths and weaknesses while assisting their companions in the same way. The Hierophant, Major Arcana V, is about the best of collective human achievement. The Five of Wands shows how we help ourselves and other individuals reach for their best and thereby add to the collective good.

You are in a competitive situation. See it for what it is: an opportunity to grow and to help others grow. Although competing with others, you are really in competition with yourself. Do your best, for your own good and for the good of others.

Be aware of inappropriate motivations. Compete with an eye to improving yourself and society, not to hurt or destroy someone else. Play by the rules. Have confidence in yourself and do not seek an unfair advantage by cheating.

Six of Wands

A man rides a horse through a cheering crowd and colorful flags. He enjoys a hero's welcome, celebrating a great victory. The Lovers, Major Arcana VI, shows the glory and joy resulting from wise and balanced choices. This man's achievements can only be the result of such well-made decisions.

You are in a position to receive outward congratulations for your actions. You have done well and deserve to be recognized. Enjoy the accolades.

Be aware of staying too long at the celebration. While it is right to celebrate achievement, do not rest too long on your laurels.

Seven of Wands

*S*tanding before a door, slightly open to the night sky, a man defends his position. Strong and brave, he faces all comers. This is not the benevolent competition of the Five of Wands; rather, it is more threatening. Like the Chariot, Major Arcana VII, he is steadfast and feels sure of his will. However, while there is control of will, there is a deeper lack of understanding, an echo of the Chariot, indicated by the night sky behind him. His actions are being questioned. While his understanding is imperfect, his convictions carry him through.

You are being asked to defend your actions or beliefs. Do not fear the attack. Use the questions raised to clarify your understanding. If your beliefs are sound, a closer examination of them will hurt nothing and will add to your wisdom.

Be aware of childish obstinacy. If you find your stance is wrong, admit defeat and refine your beliefs so that they will stand up to examination. On the other hand, do not give up the fight out of fear.

Eight of Wands

*E*ight wands fly through the sky in an orderly fashion over a peaceful pastoral scene. Already set in motion, how the wands will land is already determined. They move with a steadfast surety and speed. Just as the lion and the woman walk together with unity toward a common goal in Strength, Major Arcana VIII, so do the events in the Eight of Wands. The determined purpose and delicate balance of Strength is joined with the fiery action of Wands. Things are set to happen and they will happen quickly.

You are waiting for an outcome. You will not wait long. Events set in motion are moving speedily to their inexorable conclusion.

Be aware of the dangers of interfering. By altering the movement of one of the wands, the others, because of their proximity to each other, will be affected. The connections are intricate and you may not be able to see the larger ramifications of your actions.

Nine of Wands

A tired soldier retreats from an insurmountable blockade. He is holding himself up by his will, represented by his wand, alone. He did not expect this failure and is puzzled by this situation. His experience did not reflect his expectations. The tiny scarab to his right indicates the quiet voice of his soul. Like the Hermit of Major Arcana IX, the warrior must retreat and regroup. He must compare what he believes to his worldly experience and reconcile them.

You are caught by a failure unawares. Things did not turn out as you planned and you aren't sure why. Take time to reflect, to determine what happened and why. Learn from this situation and resume the battle.

Be aware of despair. While the situation is difficult and perhaps confusing, do not give up. Withdraw to heal and learn, not to escape life.

Ten of Wands

A purposeful man carries his large burden through the night toward the morning sky. He is almost done with his wearisome task. The full moon above and the dawn on the horizon indicate the end of a cycle. This card echoes the turning of the Wheel of Fortune, Major Arcana X. The deer watch silently from a distance, perhaps inspiring the man with their quiet strength.

You are nearly finished with an arduous task. You may be exhausted, but the light at the end of the tunnel, like a beautiful sunrise, gives you the determination to see this through. Draw on your most basic instincts for the strength to finish what you've started.

Be aware of stopping too soon. Do not let the relief of seeing the end of the situation cause you to falter; rather, let it focus your actions.

Cups

Ace of Cups

*I*dealism, romance, the Holy Grail—this gift of the universe provides depth and feeling to our lives. Here, the gift is purity of emotion, a spiritual love that is meant to guide us. If we set our eye on spirituality, we can more easily see our way through the tumultuous experience of the wide range of human emotions. Just as the moon remains the same but appears differently depending on the focus of the sun, so our experience of emotions varies according to how we choose to see them. Like the energy of the Magician, Major Arcana I, the gift of the grail is meant to guide us. But it can, like the manipulative side of the Magician, lead us down some rocky roads.

You are being drawn along by a feeling. Your emotions are engaged and you feel more alive than usual. It may be the beginning of a romance, a spiritual epiphany, or a desire to express yourself artistically. Whatever it is, you are at the start of an exciting adventure.

Be aware of running from this experience. Do not fear, discount, or avoid the intensity of your feelings. Although it may feel uncomfortable at first, learn to identify and express your emotions.

Two of Cups

$\mathcal{A}$ blond woman and a brunette man join under the shadowy light of the moon. Their union creates a unique energy that is mystical and beautiful. Just as the High Priestess, Major Arcana II, joins the poetic music of the heavenly bodies with the scientific charting of astronomy, the blond female and the brunette male unify opposing qualities. The result is as magical and intriguing as the High Priestess.

You are faced with the opportunity to partner with someone, whether it is a romantic union or a business venture. Whichever it is, the potential for creating something very special is there. Honor the gift of the moment and enjoy it.

Be aware of unrealized potential. If all the elements of a strong partnership are in place but no forward movement is made, the moment may be lost. Enjoy the magic of the moment but do not let it enslave you.

Three of Cups

$\mathcal{T}$hree women dance in the heavens, taking inspiration from the golden waters below. They are dressed in blue for Swords/Air, green for Pentacles/Earth, and red for Wands/Fire. The most graceful expressions of all the elements find inspiration from the depths of human emotion. This emotional experience binds them while allowing them to achieve their best. Like the Empress, Major Arcana III, this card shows the joy resulting from nurturing and finding joy in others.

You are surrounded by those who give you happiness. Remember to acknowledge and appreciate them. Take time with others to celebrate the simple joys of being alive.

Be aware of ignoring the simple pleasures of life and not appreciating those around you. This is not a time to focus on your problems, no matter how pressing. Practice gratitude and see what develops.

Four of Cups

A dreamy youth reclines against a tree. Although three lovely chalices sit beside him, he ignores them. He imagines something better; he is even offered something better. The squirrel in the tree and the mouse in the grass take more interest in the gift than the youth for whom it is intended. His romantic ideals may cause him to miss opportunities that he may later regret. This card echoes the negative side of the Emperor, Major Arcana IV. The desire for order and stability can lead to a quest for perfection that does not exist, causing a disdain for reality.

You not only have gifts at your disposal, you are being offered another at this moment. At the expense of current happiness, you are focusing on an idealized concept that does not exist.

Be aware of the reverse, and do not let go of healthy ideals that guide and shape your life for a shabby substitution. You must know the difference between convictions and fantasies.

Five of Cups

A man despairs over the spilling of three cups, unaware of the two glittering cups behind him. A time of mourning over a loss is natural and necessary. But if it goes on too long, it becomes a melodramatic parody. By turning to the wisdom of the Hierophant, Major Arcana V, this man can find guidance in his mourning and support in healing his heart. Then he can turn to the future, find hope in the dawning of a new day, and embrace the two cups waiting for him.

You have experienced a loss and must mourn. Turn to a wise friend or counselor, a spiritual advisor, or a religious tradition to help you heal properly so you can embrace a bright future in due time.

Be aware of prolonging your time of mourning, whether it is out of a desire for attention or fear of the future.

Six of Cups

*C*hildren explore a colorful fantasyland. Cups filled with delightful flowers and friendly animals enchant them. The cat in the foreground represents the present, and the scene behind it is the past. This memory of a happy time in the past can provide warmth, a sense of security, and an inspiration to share the same benevolence. It can also create a romanticized sense of nostalgia that causes a profound sense of disappointment in a current situation. Just as the Lovers, Major Arcana VI, indicates balanced choice, so this card contains a necessary element in choosing how the past will affect the present.

You find yourself faced with a memory. Consider it carefully, as memories can be tricky things, altered by time and distance and even current desires. Make sure that whatever role it plays in shaping your current actions is balanced by logic and reality.

Be aware of letting your past or your ideas of the past control you.

Seven of Cups

*C*ups filled with intriguing images hover over the water. They have risen out of the subconsciousness. Like sirens' voices distracting unwary sailors, these fantasies may distract travelers from their true courses. Like the focus and control of the Chariot, Major Arcana VII, a strong will is needed to overcome the distractions of the imagination.

You are faced with many choices, opportunities, and dreams. Find inspiration from them where you can. Acknowledge them as distractions if they take you from the path you have chosen.

Be aware of being overcome by the power of these distractions. They may be enticing and you enjoy entertaining them for a time, but you may regret that choice in the long run.

Eight of Cups

A young man turns his back on a tumble of cups. A sleeping mole indicates blindness. He gazes off at the horizon as if assessing the landscape before setting off on his journey. He has tasted of all the cups and found them lacking. Although they may have satiated him for a time or masked his true feelings, they really only provided a kind of diversion from what he must do. The full moon rises and he cannot ignore its light and call, just as he can no longer ignore the voice of his soul. The time for blindness is over and he must acclimate to the light and, like Strength, Major Arcana VIII, move forward with determination.

You have dallied with desires and fancies that kept you distracted from your path, from doing what you know you must. It is time to turn away from this shallow comfort and forge ahead.

Be aware of being misled by the moon. Do not mistake a desire to run from mistakes for a call from your soul. If the cups here represent a mess in your life, maybe you are meant to stay and clean it up.

Nine of Cups

In his comfortable home, an innkeeper raises his cup and salutes his comfort, abundance, and good fortune. He has invested in creating a welcoming place for others and a secure situation for himself. His fortune, represented by the barrels of beer, is that of good cheer, not necessarily of money or material gain. In Major Arcana IX, the Hermit goes off alone to solidify his knowledge and then he returns to the world to share it and help others. So this man has found his own way and hence has much to share with others, even the charming mice who play without fear of danger on the beams overhead.

You have achieved a place of comfortable abundance. You have much love and nurturing affection to give. You are happy with what you have and desire to share with others, knowing that sharing such gifts only increases them.

Be aware of taking the energy of the Hermit to the extreme. Do not enjoy your good fortune alone or hoard it. Do not indulge in a pompous sense of self-satisfaction but share what you have with graciousness.

Ten of Cups

A woman and her daughter sit in front of a cozy home. Their leisurely domestic activity and industriousness is underlined by the presence of bees, while the cat shows a playfulness along with the work. The Wheel of Fortune, Major Arcana X, has this family at the top. They have harmonious lives free of strife or conflict.

You may note the absence of a male figure. The artist created this image as if he were coming home from work to his family. The scene shows the contentment and joy he experiences.

You have created a happy home life. It is full of satisfying activities and comforts. This moment is the epitome of domestic bliss. Enjoy it.

Be aware of letting contentment turn to laziness. Do not neglect your family, thinking everything is fine. Everything *is* fine—because you've treated each other well and with tender consideration. Do not stop those behaviors.

Swords

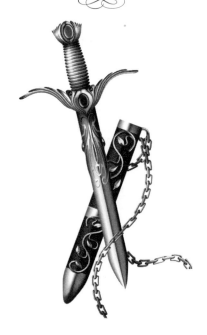

Ace of Swords

The gift of the sword is the intellect, the rational mind. This is a powerful gift and a dangerous one. The sword of truth can pierce through confusing problems. The mind, though, is complex. The way we think controls the way we perceive reality. By extension, the sword is communication; our words can heal or they can hurt. Just as the Magician, Major Arcana I, can use his will and power to create wondrous things, he can use them to confuse and play tricks on the unsuspecting as well.

You have the gift of thought. Use it rightly to see the world clearly, to communicate well, and to create a happy, healthy reality.

Be aware of having a sharp tongue. A clever wit or a desire for honesty are gifts of the sword. Do not use them in a destructive manner.

Two of Swords

A woman is blindfolded by a golden band. Two swords cross in front of the moon. The woman is experiencing conflict between her intellect and the less rational, intuitive aspects of herself. Ironically, her face seems calm, as if she is unaffected by this conflict. Perhaps she has chosen to be blinded to this situation. Unlike the High Priestess, Major Arcana II, this woman does not dance elegantly between intellect and intuition. She is unengaged, making no progress. The battle between head and heart remain unresolved.

You are faced with a decision and you aren't sure what to do. You have to decide. Remove your blindfold and look squarely at the situation. Most likely you know what to do but are afraid.

Be aware of ignoring the situation for too long. Pretending it isn't there won't make it go away.

Three of Swords

A large heart looms against a stormy sky, pierced by three swords. Clearly this is heartbreak very dramatically and tragically expressed. Consider the image carefully. The sun, representing the self, is centered on the heart. The ego is identifying entirely with the emotional distress, making it bigger than it should be. The swords embedded in the heart indicate that a way of looking at the situation is faulty. Removing the focus from the emotion allows a glimpse of the bigger picture. A proper perspective allows more clarity. In this instance, the Empress, Major Arcana III, can provide the nurturing and healing that will help transcend the heartbreak.

You have experienced a heartbreak. However, you are not seeing the effects of this heartbreak clearly. Although it is hard to end a relationship, it does not mean the end of your life . . . which is probably how you are feeling. Seek a realistic perspective.

Be aware of the lure of the role of the tragically broken-hearted lover. It gives the lover reason to pine and mourn and never move forward. It is a sham, an excuse to avoid life.

Four of Swords

A worn-out soldier finds rest in a quiet, bricked area. For the moment he is safe from battle. In this sanctuary, he can regroup. And regroup he must, as his problems are still present, as indicated by the swords. But for the moment, he can take a break and face his challenges refreshed. The benefits of the Emperor, Major Arcana IV, can be seen here. By providing a stable, secure environment, the soldier can gather his thoughts and bring his best possible efforts to the situation.

You need time to regroup. Although your situation is problematic, you will not resolve it until you can take some time out. Remove yourself from the situation, meditate, and find your center. By recharging your spiritual strength, you will bring your best efforts to solve the problem.

Be aware of ignoring the problem by distracting yourself. This is not a card of escapism, but of utilizing your spiritual foundation for renewal.

Five of Swords

$\mathscr{A}$ warrior stands victorious, carrying five swords. The dawn breaks, revealing the battered remains of his opponents. The defeated figures in the background do not emphasize the warrior's glory. Instead the image suggests a Pyrrhic victory. Although there is clearly a winner and a loser in this battle, it is not clear that the cost of winning was worth it. The Hierophant, Major Arcana V, speaks of the lessons of human history, among other things. War or any sort of devastating battle has its costs. Whether such means of control are always worth the effort is unclear. It is a lesson we have not quite sorted out.

You are at the end of a battle. Are you the winner or the loser? In either case, what was lost and what was won? Was it worth it? What have you learned from the experience?

Be aware of seeing battle as the only or the easiest way to solve disputes. The costs are high on both sides. Perhaps a more conciliatory approach would serve everyone better in the long run.

Six of Swords

$\mathscr{B}$y the light of the full moon, a woman makes her secret, silent journey by water. Where is she traveling to and what does she leave behind? Does it matter? Will her destination change anything in her life? She brings with her the way she views the world, as shown by the swords in her boat. As the saying goes, "Wherever you go, there you are." Major Arcana VI, the Lovers, is about making balanced choices. By traveling over the water (her emotions) and carrying her same thought patterns (the swords), she is making a choice, but is it a sound one? The toad seems to indicate more of a reliance on the reptilian part of the brain, from whence the "flight" impulse arises.

You are running from something. Unless you examine the way you think, your running will accomplish nothing except an immediate escape from what is troubling you. Until you learn to face it, it will come up again in some other guise.

Be aware of overanalyzing. Our ancient instincts exist as a defense mechanism. Although probably not as often now, there are times when fleeing a dangerous situation is the right thing to do.

Seven of Swords

A shady character carrying five swords retreats from a building. He apparently intended to disarm an enemy. His plan, though, seems spontaneous and foolhardy. He cannot even take away all the swords. There is every likelihood that his action will so anger his enemy that one of those swords he left behind will find its way into his back. Unlike the discipline and willpower of the Chariot, Major Arcana VII, this character responded to his situation in an illogical and dangerous fashion.

You are faced with a problem. Worse than that, you are considering a poor plan for solving it. Reconsider your solution and try to find one that will yield a more satisfactory result.

Be aware of impetuousness. Your actions have consequences and you would do well to consider them before acting.

Eight of Swords

A woman, blindfolded and chained, is surrounded by swords. Her situation is at the same time simple and complex. The blindfold shows her confusion, her inability to see clearly. The chains represent her inability to move, although they seem to be merely wrapped loosely around her wrists. It would seem a simple task to let the chain drop, remove the blindfold, and escape through the spaces between the swords. It is, however, her own thoughts that keep her bound. The swords are her mind, surrounding her and keeping her blind and immobile. Unlike Major Arcana VIII, Strength, which has tamed the sometimes frightening animal aspects of ourselves and can consequently walk with courage, this woman is controlled by fear.

You feel helpless. You cannot see; you cannot move; you sense danger all around you. The situation is entirely of your own making. The good news is that if you made it, you can unmake it. You have the ability to see things clearly, you just need the courage to do so.

Be aware of giving in to a sense of helplessness. Do not give up your power. Take control of your life. Do not let fear bind and blind you.

Nine of Swords

By the light of a crescent moon, a woman sits up in bed as if awakened by a bad dream. An owl peers forward as nine swords float above her head. She crosses her arms across her chest as if to protect her heart. As evidenced by the swords, this woman is clearly troubled by some large problem, large enough to disturb her sleep. The owl, a symbol of wisdom, is nearby, apparently ready to share its knowledge and thereby impart some comfort to the woman. As she puzzles out the problem, perhaps she will see her way clear to wisdom and truth. For now, though, she is alone and closed off. This is the Hermit, Major Arcana IX, taken to a sad extreme. In this time of trial, she would do well to reach out and get the comfort and wisdom she needs. It seems that it is near at hand.

You are agonizing over something. For whatever reason you are working through this alone, even though help is nearby. Reach out and allow someone to guide and comfort you.

Be aware of isolation. You may feel like you're alone or your pride may stop you from reaching out. You're not alone and your pride may cost you more than you know.

Ten of Swords

*F*rom the dark shadows, a deer looks on the body of a man lying on the ground. It is a poignant and strange sight. While the man may very well be dead, there is a peacefulness about the scene. The ten swords above him illuminate the scene with a radiant glow. Whatever hardship he has lived through, he is at the end of it. In terms of the Wheel of Fortune, Major Arcana X, this man is at the bottom and is about to start a new cycle.

You are at the end of a hard situation. It is probably about all you can stand and you may not think you'll make it. You can. Have faith that the tide is about to turn.

Be aware of losing hope. Do not give up. The Wheel is about to begin an upward turn.

Pentacles

Ace of Pentacles

$\mathcal{T}$his is a gift of resources—likely money, raw materials, or time. It is probably the most straightforward of the suits. For that reason, the gifts of Pentacles are not always as highly esteemed as the other suits' gifts, or sometimes they are overvalued and lead to greed for material wealth or obsession with sensuous living. Whatever form the gift takes, it up to us—as the weasel reminds us here and like the Magician, Major Arcana I—to use our skill and determination to make something worthwhile of it.

You have been given a resource. Use it well and be grateful.

Be aware of the temptation to undervalue or squander this gift because you consider it mundane and not a true gift of the universe.

Two of Pentacles

$\mathcal{O}$n the shore, a man balances two pentacles. The mastery and ease of his skill creates a rainbow, making the act seem magical. The representation of the other suits—the dolphin (intelligence/Swords), water (Cups), and fiery light of the rainbow (Wands)—indicates a deep overall balance that allows for this easy control of everyday life. Like the High Priestess, Major Arcana II, existing between poetry and science, this gentleman dances through life juggling work and joy.

You have a full life and the ability to keep every-thing flowing. You make it seem easy. You find satis-faction in not only doing many things and doing them well, but also in not making your busyness into a com-petition.

Be aware of overdoing for the sake of the admira-tion of others. Don't judge yourself and others by how much you do, and don't seek achievement at the ex-pense of quality and overall happiness.

Three of Pentacles

A master craftsman alone with his forge finds great pleasure in admiring his work. It is more than simple pride, although that is part of it. He experiences the sensual pleasure of well-crafted work and acknowledges the hidden magic in the creation of physical items.

Of all the threes, he is the closest to Major Arcana III, the Empress. Like her, he creates and delights in the creation; he loves the process and the product.

You have a skill that gives you great satisfaction. It is something you love to do, and you find great plea-sure in the end result.

Be aware of losing the magical connection to process and product. If you find that something that used to delight you has become rote, try to recapture your early feelings or maybe pursue a new activity.

Four of Pentacles

A man in rich purple robes embroidered with gold grips four pentacles in his arms. He has taken pleasure in achieving monetary worth. But money is an abstraction, a representation for things necessary to life or that give life beauty and pleasure. He has lost track of that and so he stands alone in his cold pride, neither sharing his bounty nor even really enjoying it himself. He reflects an extreme of Major Arcana IV, the Emperor. When the Emperor provides order for the betterment of life, all is well. When he imposes order for order's sake, life becomes sterile.

You possess a certain amount of resources, and you've become possessive of them. You are hoarding your money, your time, your abilities. You've lost sight of what these things are for and you face a lonely, unfulfilled future unless you use your resources wisely.

Be aware of the opposite extreme of giving away all you have so that you are depleted and have nothing left to offer.

Five of Pentacles

B efore a colorful stained-glass window stand a man and a woman with a child. The man holds his hat with a humble attitude. The tired, hungry child clutches his mother, who holds out her hands helplessly. They are in desperate need. The beautiful window with the light shining through it does not seem to yield any answers for them. In the Hierophant, Major Arcana V, we saw a stained-glass window, a representation of the achievements of humankind. All the glorious structures and achievements in the world are meaningless, though, if they do not provide guidance, help, or inspiration.

You are in need. Help is nearby. Do not be dissuaded even if the building, organization, or person seems imposing. Ask for the help you need.

Be aware of making your need larger than it is. Learn what resources are available to help you help yourself.

Six of Pentacles

A rich man stands, with scales in hand, happily measuring out pentacles. Outside his window, hands clutch and reach but do not grasp the pentacles falling near them. The rich man seems willing enough to give, but does not pay attention to where he is giving. He lets resources fall by the wayside and does not attend to the need directly outside his window. Unlike the Lovers in Major Arcana VI, he is not making balanced choices. He is squandering his gifts while deluding himself that he is charitable.

You give of your resources freely, but are you paying attention to what you are doing? Are you giving people what they need or just what it pleases you to give?

Be aware of proud but dispassionate giving. Giving your child a new computer when he really wants your attention is not a good use of your resources, nor is it helpful to your child.

Seven of Pentacles

A woman with a basket stands by a tree laden with pentacles. The sheep in the field watch her while a squirrel considers trying to make off with one of the pentacles. Like the Chariot, Major Arcana VII, this woman has exerted her will and control to make this tree fruitful. However, she is going a step beyond the Chariot. She is assessing her investment to see if the yield matches her expectations and was worth the effort she put into it.

You have sown seeds of some sort. They are bearing fruit and it is time for the harvest. Take time to compare the investment with the results. If it is not what you'd hoped, determine what you can do differently next time.

Be aware of being so excited about the harvest that you neglect the balance sheet.

Eight of Pentacles

A lonely apprentice works late into the night on his project. He is focused and determined, perhaps too focused to notice his little companion. Like Major Arcana VIII, Strength, this young man tamed his baser instincts and desires in order to achieve something greater. Even though he may wish to go out and enjoy himself, he is willing to forgo immediate pleasure for the sake of a long-term goal.

You are involved in a course of study in preparation for a better future. Your discipline and drive will serve you well. Do take a moment, though, and enjoy some pleasant companionship.

Be aware of driving yourself too hard and to the exclusion of all else. Even in the midst of heavy studies, a person needs a little rest and relaxation.

Nine of Pentacles

An accomplished woman stands by her gazebo. She gazes on her noble falcon with pride and is surrounded by a garden of plentiful pentacles. She has a right to be proud because she has achieved this luxurious lifestyle on her own. Like the Hermit, Major Arcana IX, she has chosen a life alone, which she does not seem to mind at all.

You have accomplished much that makes you proud. You have created a life that you enjoy and that satisfies you. In spite of your choices, you do not feel lonely.

Be aware that you may have been happy and not lonely, but there may come a time when that changes. Don't be afraid to change your lifestyle and find someone special to share it with.

Ten of Pentacles

A wooden chest of pentacles lies under a tree. A ferret peers over the edge curiously. A turtle makes his slow way past, rather unconcerned with the whole affair. Whose chest is this? Why is it unattended and open? Aren't they afraid someone will take them? Evidently the owner isn't too concerned. Since this is a ten, it reflects the Wheel of Fortune, Major Arcana X, and the end of a cycle. Whoever owns this chest probably left it for someone else to find. That has a nice, unified feel to it: they left a chest of pentacles to repay the universe for the single pentacle given to them long ago in the form of the Ace of Pentacles.

You have reached the end of a cycle. You've learned all you care to learn, you've invested all you want, you're ready to move on to something new. Just as you received a gift to start off, why not share your abundance with someone else?

Be aware of holding on to things when you'll never use them again. The tennis racket was great while you played—now pass it on to someone new.

THE
Court Cards

*T*he Major Arcana illustrate the major milestones in our lives. The Minor Arcana show everyday events. In a sense, these cards set the stage. Although the court cards are part of the Minor Arcana, they play a different role. The court cards are like the actors on that stage. They provide personality, representing either other people involved or aspects of ourselves. In addition, Pages sometimes indicate messages. To learn more about the personalities and meanings of the court cards, see *Understanding the Tarot Court* by Mary K. Greer and Tom Little.

Exercise 11

*M*ake up a question or situation. Lay out your court cards and imagine how each one would answer the question or advise you in the situation.

Pages

Page of Wands

A young man cautiously carries a wand. He is a little stiff, as if this were a new experience and he wants to get everything just right. Although careful, he is not nervous or anxious. He has prepared for this moment as much as possible and is filled with confidence.

You are ready to try something new. It may be something you've thought about for some time or have been reading or studying. It's time to put your thoughts into action. You're well prepared, so go ahead and take the next step.

Be aware of jumping into something you're not ready for. If you haven't laid the groundwork, you'll probably be surprised by unexpected events or expenses.

The Page of Wands can indicate a message, usually pertaining to your career, a project you're working on, or a course of study you are interested in.

Page of Cups

A young man holds a goblet with apparent carelessness. He adopts a posture of ease and almost of superiority and defiance. He is facing a moment of truth and is convinced that he knows best.

You are experiencing an emotional situation, one that you probably don't have much experience with. You have the strength of your convictions and present an imperturbable face to the outside world. However, because of your lack of experience, you may feel a little apprehension under your confident mask.

Be aware of assuming you know everything and ignoring advice. Emotions are surprising things. Even if you think you are prepared, realize that you more than likely haven't considered everything. Don't shun the advice of someone more experienced.

The Page of Cups can indicate a message, usually pertaining to a romance, a creative or artistic project, or an emotionally charged situation.

Page of Swords

A young man attempts to stand confidently and proudly. He tries to express a sense of disinterest, as though he's done this a thousand times before. His face, though he doesn't know it, shows more apprehension than he'd like it to. Who wouldn't be a little nervous? He does have a very large (and potentially dangerous) sword and although he knows how to wield it in theory, he hasn't actually used it.

You are ready to face a new challenge. The theory and logic is clear to you; you have all the tools you need; you know exactly what to do and how to do it. Yet you feel inexplicably scared. Your fear isn't unusual, though. There is no substitute for experience— and that is something you don't have at this point. Know that regardless of the outcome, you will have done the best you possibly can.

Be aware of overanalyzing. Swords are the suit of the intellect, so there is the danger of thinking about something so much that you become paralyzed with worry.

The Page of Swords can indicate a message, usually pertaining to a current problem, issue, or belief system.

Page of Pentacles

A young man holds a pentacle. He appears almost bored. Although not an adept by any means, he does have enough experience to start playing with technique. He does not carefully hold the pentacle, instead he barely holds it, as if to see how little he needs to touch it yet still keep it in place. He is definitely ready for the next level.

You have been practicing something and are already quite good at it. Your studies are beginning to manifest into actual completed projects. You are ready to present your work to the outside world. Perhaps it's time to consider something more complicated and challenging.

Be aware of becoming careless. Although you do have skill, you lack the experience that allows one to perform almost mindlessly. Also, be careful of stagnation. Once you master this level, continue to challenge yourself and don't become lazy.

The Page of Pentacles can indicate a message, usually pertaining to a project you've completed, finances, or resources.

Knights

Knight of Wands

A fully armored knight rides confidently and purposefully along. His stance and coloring indicate passion and bravery. He is well rested and ready to take adventure where he finds it.

Your passion is moving you ahead very quickly. Whatever you are facing, you are very excited about it. You feel no fear, although you are certainly feeling a heady adrenaline rush. You are ready for a grand adventure. If one doesn't come to you, you will go out and find it.

Be aware of recklessness. Remember "Fools—and the Knight of Wands—rush in where angels fear to tread." Just be careful.

Knight of Cups

A high-spirited knight and his horse prance around in the twilight. He holds his goblet up high. This knight is clearly ready for celebrating or wooing a fair maiden rather than fighting. Governed by the suit of Cups, this knight is dreamy and romantic. Appearances and ambiance mean as much to him as skill and bravery. He can wield a poetic phrase as well as his sword.

You are feeling very romantic. You are more interested in candles, decadent dinners, and lofty declarations of love than usual. Celebrating the beautiful and sensual experiences of life is just as necessary as any other experience. Enjoy!

Be aware of daydreaming when you shouldn't. Don't let romantic ideals take you away from your path. It's one thing to celebrate a dream-come-true feeling in your life; it's another to chase after dreams that can never be.

Knight of Swords

*H*ere is the quintessential questing knight. He holds his energetic steed in check as he dramatically lifts his sword—he is ready for action. Since Swords are ruled by the intellect, it makes sense that his quest is overseen by an owl, a bird often associated with wisdom. He has turned his back on everything except his quarry. He is focused and committed. Nothing better get in his way.

You are in the midst of something. You know exactly what you want to do and precisely how you are going to do it. You are very single-minded right now. Your goal is in sight.

Be aware of being so focused that you miss new developments in the situation. Pay attention to what is going on around you. There is a danger of ignoring or being insensitive to those around you.

Knight of Pentacles

*M*ore than the other knights, this one is in a defensive posture. He has been through battles and adventures and is probably ready to rest awhile. Although not in the middle of a battle, this knight is alert and diligent. He will always guard himself and whatever or whomever else needs protecting.

You have fought some battles and enjoyed some adventures. Now you'd like to rest and regroup, maybe spend some time enjoying quieter, more domestic scenes. Take some time off and make yourself feel safe, if necessary. You may need to adopt a protective or defensive stance.

Be aware of resting on your laurels or stagnating. If you had a traumatic experience, do not let it paralyze you or become an excuse for not moving forward.

Queens

Queen of Wands

𝒜 serene but alert woman guards a pillar topped with flames. She holds her wand in a calmly protective fashion in front of the pillar. She is not only ready for action, but actively scanning the horizon, seeking it out.

Your passion is quietly contained, ready to burst out at any minute. You are seeking an outlet for your energy. This may be in the form of a new project of your own or helping someone with an exciting undertaking. You love activity for its own sake, and you are not adverse to public admiration as a result of your skills and brilliant personality.

Be aware of ego and the desire for advancement, be it social or career related. Although you are a true and loyal friend, your ego can get in the way.

Queen of Cups

A romantic-looking woman gazes into the distance, seeing something as if in a dream. Slightly tragic in her moody environment, she almost has the look of an ill-fated princess in a fairy tale or a woman deeply concerned for the welfare of others.

Your heart is engaged, whether in deep concern for loved ones or about your own emotional well-being. Although things around you may not seem perfect, there is a sensual beauty to the situation. Perhaps you are concerned about the longevity of a relationship (romantic or otherwise). Look to the needs of your heart.

Be aware of becoming bewitched by your own emotions. Do not let them overshadow reality to such an extent that you don't see what's really going on. Be careful in your concern for others. Sometimes people have to make their own mistakes. They may be in danger of being smothered by your overly attentive care.

Queen of Swords

A confident woman stands with her sword poised but not threatening. Light glints off her sword and crown, showing a relationship between truth (the light of the sun), her thoughts (her crown), and her actions (her sword). She is slightly on guard but not so much that she is fearful of the world.

You have used your mind, truth, and logical thinking to create order in your world. You've taken your suffering and joys and married them to a useful philosophy so that you are at ease in the world. You are a good and helpful friend, although some may say you lack emotion.

Be aware of depending too much on order. Remember to be flexible when things don't go your way. Allow others to behave as they believe right. Your ways are not everyone's ways. Do not divorce yourself from your emotions in an effort to protect yourself.

Queen of Pentacles

A stately woman holds a pentacle with quiet pride. Her face is self-satisfied, almost (but not quite) smug. Like the Queen of Swords, she has a strong, self-contained confidence.

You have worked hard and well. You have created a life filled with physical pleasures and beauty through your skills and careful budgeting of resources. You take great pride in your practicality. People around you enjoy the fruits of your labor. And although this gives you pleasure, you get just as much satisfaction from the results of your endeavors.

Be aware of becoming fixated on end results and losing all joy in the process of creating. There is a danger of worrying about money too much. While it's wise to be careful, don't become obsessed with frugality. And don't sacrifice your spiritual, creative, and emotional life on the altar of practicality.

Kings

King of Wands

A strong-willed man sits comfortably in his throne gazing at his flame-tipped wand. He is mesmerized by it, to the exclusion of all else.

You are focused, determined, and driven. Something has your full attention and you are channeling all your energy and skills in that direction. You have a strong sense that you are right in all things concerning this venture. Your ambition or social needs are engaged. For now, that is all that matters.

Be aware of believing that you are right, that your way is the only way. There is a danger of becoming overly bossy or intolerant of others.

King of Cups

A slightly melancholy king lounges on his throne, staring at his cup. Although he has much power, he seems to be missing something.

You are fortunate in your achievements. You have accomplished much, and built a good business or career for yourself. Perhaps you have a stable, loving family life. These things give you much satisfaction, but there is a longing in your heart. It is as if in gaining power and accomplishments, you have lost touch with your creative side. Seek an artistic or creative outlet, and nurture your emotions.

Be aware of focusing on what you don't have. If you look at only the things that are missing in your life (such as personal, creative projects), you can grow bitter and resentful. You may neglect your existing obligations if you give in to pouting and self-obsession rather than workable solutions.

King of Swords

*A*n appealing man half-sits on his throne, leaning heavily on his sword. The sword seems to be more support than the throne. He is a charismatic man, exuding confidence, intelligence, and power.

Your intelligence is at the core of your persona. You have used it well to create a successful life for yourself and those associated with you. Your wisdom benefits others and you are comfortable sharing your ideas and opinions.

Be aware of letting your intelligence define you in full. Seek a bit more balance in your own self-image and your dealings with others. Be careful, too, of becoming a snob. Your mind is powerful but, if turned inward too much, you may be prone to paranoia.

King of Pentacles

A listless man sits impatiently on his throne. He's gazing into the distance and not paying any attention to his environment. He holds his staff loosely, as if he doesn't care if he wields it or not.

You enjoy the finer things in life and are willing to work hard for them. Although you want the best, you don't expect it handed to you. At this point, you have worked hard and long; you've wielded your authority and talent wisely. You would like to set down responsibility, if even for just a while, and indulge yourself in the good things life has to offer.

Be aware of becoming lazy or dependent on material possessions. Your love of luxury could overcome your practical nature and lead to debt. Although you may be seduced by the good life, you'll find that it alone cannot satisfy you.

THE
Spreads

     *S*preads provide the framework for the answers, information, and advice you seek. Your question will help determine the spread you'll use. Before you start, look at the five spreads in this chapter and select the most appropriate. If none here fit the situation, try pulling one card for it or try making up a spread.

Exercise 12

     *P*ractice designing a spread. Imagine that a friend has an opportunity to take a trip at a great price. She doesn't have the money on hand and would have to borrow it (probably using her credit card). The trip is one she's wanted to take for some time. She wants help in deciding whether or not to go. What spread would you design?

The Three-Card Spread

The three-card spread has many variations and is adaptable to many situations. Some of the most common variants are:

The Past, Present, Future Spread

*U*se this spread to get a picture of how a situation came into being and what is the most likely outcome if everything stays as it is. By examining the past and present energy, you can work to facilitate the possible outcome or find ways to alter that course.

1. Past Influences

2. Present Situation

3. Future Possibilities

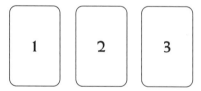

The Body, Mind, Spirit Spread

*T*his spread is useful when you feel a bit out of balance and want to pinpoint the area that needs attention. It's kind of a holistic thermometer. Once you've determined the problem, you can either do another spread to find options to address the issue or simply pull a single card for advice.

1. Body

2. Mind

3. Spirit

Choices Spread

*W*hen you have a dilemma, situation, or question with two distinct choices, use this spread to help get a clear picture. From it you can sometimes find facets of the dilemma you hadn't considered before, and ramifications of each choice. If you still feel unclear, pull a fourth, random card to indicate a third choice you may not have thought of yet.

1. Dilemma or question

2. Choice A

3. Choice B

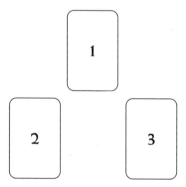

Celtic Cross Spread

*T*his spread is very popular; it can simply and clearly assess a problem, what caused the problem, and what the outcome may be. It is limiting in that it does not provide information on how to change the outcome. The Celtic Cross spread can be a useful starting point. Once you've seen the snapshot of the situation, you can use the cards to gain more detail or insight.

There are many variations on this spread, but the one below is very common.

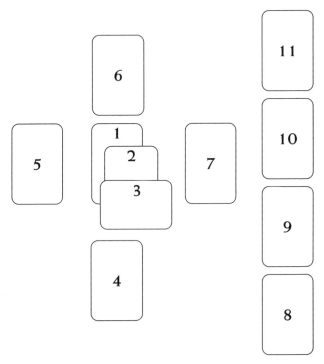

Briefly, here are the meanings of the positions:

1. SIGNIFICATOR (optional): The significator is considered optional by many readers (see page 23 for information on significators).

2. YOU: This card represents you in relation to the question.

3. CROSSING: This card indicates the conflict.

4. FOUNDATION: The card here will illustrate the basis of the problem or issue.

5. PAST: Here you will find significant influences from the past that shape the current problem.

6. PRESENT: The present forces affecting the situation.

7. FUTURE: Here are forces that will affect the outcome.

8. YOURSELF: This card is your self-image, which may be different from the "you" in card two. Self-image does not always reflect the inner you.

9. ENVIRONMENT: This is how others see you in this situation.

10. HOPES AND FEARS: Here is the card illustrating either what you most hope for or most fear.

11. OUTCOME: This card indicates the probable outcome, if all things remain as they are at the moment of the reading.

The Spreads

♦

If any card in the spread puzzles you, you can pull another card from the deck as a clarifier. Be clear about what you want clarified when you draw the card. For example, if the card in the Hopes and Fears position puzzles you, determine what exactly you want to know. Do you want to know more about the fear? Do you want to know how you can best overcome the fear? Remember, the question asked is important; if you are uncertain about what you are seeking, your reading may feel muddled or ambiguous.

Another technique that can be helpful is to take the card in question and set it aside. Shuffle the rest of the deck and pull three cards, again being clear in your mind about what information you want from the tarot.

Daily Spread

$\mathcal{D}$esigned by Kathie Vyvyan and used with permission. Kathie created the daily spread because she wanted a simple spread that wasn't too overwhelming to do every day but that was specific enough to give her in-depth answers and reflections.

In addition to being a great daily spread, it is also a handy tool to help learn the cards and hone your tarot-reading skills. Kathie does this reading each morning, noting the cards selected and her interpretations in her journal. She tries to predict events that might happen based on the cards. At night, she uses a different color pen and compares what actually happened with her predictions.

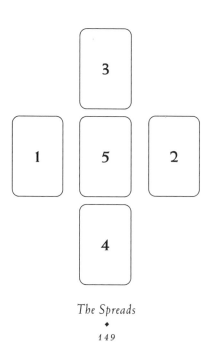

1. WORKS: Pertains to things you accomplish in a day (whether at a job or personal tasks).

2. HOME: Reflects people and activities connected with your home and home life.

3. UNEXPECTED: Indicates surprises and unexpected events.

4. YOUR ROLE: Represents your mood, actions, or reactions to events and people that fill your day.

5. OUTCOME: Shows the outcome of the day; often predicts a lesson learned or a spiritual revelation.

To Write to the Author or Artist

*I*f you wish to contact the author or artist, or would like more information about this kit, please write to the author or artist in care of Llewellyn Worldwide and we will forward your request. The author, artist, and publisher appreciate hearing from you and learning of your enjoyment of this book and how it has helped you. Llewellyn Worldwide cannot guarantee that every letter written to the author or artist can be answered, but all will be forwarded. Please write to:

Barbara Moore / Ciro Marchetti
℅ Llewellyn Worldwide
2143 Wooddale Drive, Dept. 978-0-7387-0520-0
Woodbury, MN 55125-2989, U.S.A.
Please enclose a self-addressed stamped envelope for reply,
or $1.00 to cover costs. If outside U.S.A., enclose
international postal reply coupon.

Many of Llewellyn's authors have websites with additional information and resources. For more information, please visit our website:

HTTP://WWW.LLEWELLYN.COM

Black Velvet Tarot Bag

100% cotton velvet with purple satin lining and matching drawstring and tassels. Sized to fit large and small decks.

Use this beautifully plush bag to carry and protect any of your treasured oracles: tarot cards, Tattwa cards, runes, rune cards, and more.

0-7387-0208-0

$12.95